D1733556

TOOLS FOR THE TRADE

IMPROVING STUDENT ACHIEVEMENT THROUGH THE CREATION OF RELATIONSHIPS

A Critical Race Theory Counterstory

DORA DOME, Esq.

Foreword by
ERIC K. YAMAMOTO

Fred T. Korematsu Professor of Law and Social Justice
William S. Richardson School of Law, University of Hawaii

Contents

Foreward

Eric K. Yamamoto
Fred T. Korematsu Professor of Law and Social Justice William S. Richardson School of Law, University of Hawaii
February 14, 2020

Dora Dome is the consummate educator/lawyer/humanist. Her dedicated work over many years uplifts youth mainly in the public schools, particularly those struggling at society's margins. She does this by tackling tough subjects – with forthrightness and heart. Along with her educator sister Nancy Dome, she opens minds and doors for teachers, parents, administrators and advocates and for students themselves. Lectures and hands-on training sessions are bolstered by her writings, including her books on Student Discipline, Special Education and Anti-Bullying.

Dora's new book, *"Improving Student Achievement Through the Creation of Relationships,"* expands and deepens her insightful offerings. Improving Student Achievement is a readily accessible and compelling "account of my schooling and the impact, both positive and negative, that teachers and school had on my academic achievement, as well as social and emotional growth." Through the lens of Critical Race Theory and Dora's life vignettes as a bright, talented yet struggling student ("born a poor Black child") in inner-city public schools, the book takes on the impact of stereotyping and implicit bias on student academic learning and social growth. It also reveals ways in which building real relationships among dedicated educators, coaches, family member and marginalized youths can enable those students – through grit, self-knowledge and support – to begin to transcend seemingly intractable barriers, one step at a time.

A key foundation for building genuine relationships, the book shows, is willingness of educators, parents and institutions to do the hard work of their own deeper learning about "meaningful and culturally relevant alternative[s] to the traditional...education that often [leaves students] feeling invisible and further marginalized." In some settings, this might entail learning about slavery and Jim Crow segregation, "the civil rights movement, indigenous peoples, immigration and citizenship and racial reparations" and more.

At bottom, Dora's new book leads us to conclude that "to improve academic achievement, and general well-being for students of color [and those who feel marginalized], educators must first acknowledge, then examine, the significance of politics, economics and race on the educational experiences and opportunities of [those] students."

This short yet compelling book, particularly in conjunction with educational/training sessions, opens minds and hearts with an eye toward uplifting students in need. For what "we need from our schools are experiences that are so full of wonder of life, so full of connectedness, so embedded in the context of our communities…that all of us, teachers and students alike, can learn to live lives that leave us truly satisfied."

Preface

Improving Student Achievement Through the Creation of Relationships: A Critical Race Theory Counter-Story started out as a keynote address at the 2010 Association of California School Administrator (ACSA) Leadership Conference. I had been asked to present a keynote for the "diversity" strand of the conference. At the time, I had never done a keynote and, while I was very comfortable conducting legal and equity trainings, the idea of standing on a stage and speaking to a room of people about myself was terrifying. I considered declining, but my sister Dr. Nancy Dome basically told me that it was a wonderful opportunity, both professionally and personally, and to get over myself and do it. (Although, she did not say it quite as nicely!) :)

I decided to accept the speaking engagement, but I got stressed out all over again about what to say. Not only was I worried about what to say, I questioned if I really had anything of value to share and keep people interested. Nancy and I had recently begun to work together, combining our areas of expertise, Law and Equity, in an effort to get school districts to proactively begin tackling issues of equity in their schools. As a result, I had begun re-educating myself on various topics in the areas of race and equity. In response to my readings, I found myself reflecting on my own educational experiences through the lens of the CRT framework. It was enlightening, to say the least, to discover language that accurately described my life experiences and allowed me to speak with others about those experiences using common terminology.

Once I got over my initial jitters (and cracking voice), the keynote went exceptionally well and I received a standing ovation from an audience of approximately 80 people. My relief was palpable. To my surprise, I saw people in the audience wiping tears from their eyes, while many others approached me afterwards to give me a hug and to thank me for sharing my story. In that moment I felt seen, for the challenges I experienced and success that I had achieved, and validated in a way that I had not anticipated when I embarked on writing and presenting the keynote. To be able to tell my story and have it move people in the way that it did, more powerfully than anything else I had experienced to date, illustrated to me the power of story-telling.

I have since given my keynote more times than I can count over the past 10 years. It has even evolved into a multi-media presentation, complete with then and now pictures of my teachers, all of whom remain a part of my life to this day, 40+ years later. These long-standing relationships are the most telling fact about the significance of the commitment these adults made to my kid self and to many other kids like me.

This book is dedicated to all the educators who saw beyond my challenges, believed in me, and made it their business to ensure that I succeeded: Mrs. Kent, Mrs. Ida Peoples, Mr. Dennis Flynn, Mrs. Lois Keithley, Ms. Pam Easter, Mr. Greg Miyata, Mr. Dennis Furlong, Mrs. Linda Fadler, Professor Jeffrey Prager, Professor Eric Yamamoto, Professor Amy Kastely, and Ms. Violet Palmer. Thank you all for caring!

It is my hope that in publishing my counter-story, educators near and far can hear my voice, and appreciate that my experience is one shared by hundreds of thousands of children. I hope that my story can help motivate educators to critically examine the institutional structures that perpetuate inequity and disparate outcomes for our children of color and consider how they may transform their practices to meet the needs of all children.

Dora Dome

Oakland, California, 2020

IMPROVING STUDENT ACHIEVEMENT THROUGH THE CREATION OF RELATIONSHIPS

A Critical Race Theory Counter-Story

"Improving Student Achievement Through the Creation of Relationships," is the story of my schooling and the impact, both positive and negative, that teachers, school staff, and adults had on my academic achievement as well as my social and emotional growth. While you will read examples that are disturbing, sad, and possibly guilt inducing, the purpose of my story is not to make anyone feel guilty or closed down. Quite the contrary, the reason I have chosen to share my story is because I believe teachers and adults on campus can, and do, have a significant impact, not only on the educational achievement of their students, but on their social and emotional well-being.

I have chosen to share my story because I believe in the importance of having school personnel who know their students, who will greet the students at the door or on the playground and ask about their weekend, adults who believe in their ability to succeed both academically and personally, and adults who will put them in check when they behave inappropriately and fail to meet the high expectations set for them. I hope to illustrate with my story the potential devastation that can result when a teacher doesn't believe in a child's potential and erects barriers to that child's success. I also hope to illustrate the beauty of watching a child blossom and exceed all expectations because she had a handful of adults who believed in her and refused to allow her to give up or fail.

As you read my story, I ask that you keep your mind open to the legitimacy of my experiences and of the stories that I share. Don't write them off as the exception, or the story of just one person. My story is not exceptional; there are thousands of kids like me. Many of them are waiting for someone like you to take an interest in them, to believe in them and to help them believe in themselves.

I believe that to achieve true equity in schools for all students, school districts must proactively address issues of equity. More specifically, districts must address equity issues that impact student achievement, well-being, and perpetuate stereotypic notions about who your students are and what they are capable of. As I think about how best to convey my thoughts and understandings of equity and inclusivity in our public schools, memories of my own educational experiences come to mind. Through my personal stories, I hope to illustrate the ways in which I was included, respected and cherished during my educational experience, as well as the ways in which I was marginalized, made invisible, and diminished.

My stories span my entire educational career and include present day stories from my work with school districts on equity issues. While many of my stories take place in higher education, and some in park gyms, I believe the lessons to be learned are relevant at all educational levels. This is my counter-story.

Counter-storytelling is one of the tenets of Critical Race Theory or "CRT." CRT is a reaction to long-standing legal formalism that treats law as a science and hence as necessarily neutral and objective. However, law is anything but neutral and objective. CRT is based on legal realism and acknowledges the significance of politics and economics in the way law is created, interpreted, applied, and enforced. CRT teaches, therefore, the importance of contextual analysis: examining real social conditions, power relationships, who makes the rules and enforces them and with what practical consequences.

Similarly, a contextual analysis is equally important to understanding the underlying social conditions that often lead to the underachievement and negative experiences of students of color in education. It is for this reason that I have chosen to make my thematic points utilizing the pillars of CRT. As I share my counter-story, I will also reference several other tenets of CRT, specifically the tenets of "The Permanence of Racism," "Whiteness as Property," "Interest Convergence," and "Critique of Liberalism." By using the tenets of CRT to examine my schooling, I hope to provide a way to illustrate the subtlety, complexity and pervasiveness of racism and how it manifests in educational institutions.

Counter-Story Telling/Voice of Color

The counter-story, as discussed by Mari Matsuda,

Law Professor and credited among the originators of CRT, is the *narrative that often goes untold, but is necessary to understand the experiences of students of color and to challenge the normalized dialogues that perpetuate racial stereotypes.* You will hear examples of teaching practices that were effective and culturally relevant and some that were woefully ineffective at educating a pretty bright, often challenging, definitely stubborn and strong-willed Black child. It is my hope that my counter-story will inspire you to continue to think critically about race and the impact of racism on the educational experiences of and opportunities for students of color in your schools.

I will begin my counter-story with a quote by Steve Martin made during the opening scene of the 1970's movie *The Jerk.* "I was born a poor Black child." Those of you who saw the movie will appreciate the irony of this statement, made by a white, blonde-haired man who was adopted as an infant into a Black family. Steve Martin's character grows up with his Black family, always feeling he was a little different, but never fully understanding what was different about him.

Like Steve Martin's character, I was born a poor Black child. However, I did not realize that I was "different" until the age of five. From birth to four, my family lived in the Crenshaw neighborhood of Los Angeles. The Crenshaw neighborhood in 1966 was a predominately Black neighborhood, located a couple of miles west of Watts. When I went to pre-school, my classmates were also poor and Black. We had a Black teacher, Ms. Kent, who cherished each and every one of us. Ms. Kent expected that each of us would behave and that each of us would learn at a high level. She provided us with the supports we needed to learn, told us we were smart, and did not accept excuses for mediocrity. I looked forward to school every day, because I wanted to make Ms. Kent smile and tell me how proud she was of me.

I was raised until the age of 12 by my grandmother. She also raised my twin sister and my three older brothers. She was definitely old school! She was very strict and would slap you upside your head in a heartbeat for doing something she considered disrespectful, such as rolling your eyes or not listening when you were spoken to. We won't even talk about what would happen if you actually opened your mouth and talked back!

My grandmother had a high school education and the six of us essentially lived on her social security checks from my deceased grandfather. My grandmother expected us to go to school, get decent grades and stay out of trouble. She never spoke to us about college or any other higher educational goals beyond getting a high school diploma. In retrospect, the only reason I can think of for her lack of talking to us about college was that it was so far removed from her reality that it just never occurred to her that college would be an option for us.

When I was five, we moved into what is now West Hollywood, but in 1971was still an unincorporated section of Los Angeles and the location of a large Jewish community. The first thing I noticed as we drove into our new neighborhood was that none of the kids playing outside were Black. I thought it was strange, but it was too early to understand how that fact would completely change how I would grow to perceive myself. I learned very quickly that I was different because of the color of my skin. What took a bit longer to learn was how that difference, the color of my skin, would impact the way my new teachers would conceive of my ability, my capacity to learn, and my potential for success.

As I stated earlier, I was a pretty bright, often challenging, and definitely stubborn and willful child. Not much has changed: I'm just a bit older! Over the course of the first few years at my new school, I learned that my new teachers were no Ms. Kent. It was clear that they did not expect much from me by the way they spoke to me in class and by the way they responded to the work I produced. I lost interest in trying to achieve because I did not see the excitement in their eyes when I did well.

Several years ago, I looked at my report cards from my elementary school years and the clear pattern throughout those seven years was high marks for the first reporting period and my grades gradually and consistently going down for the rest of the school year to a solidly average level. I recall starting each school year a little anxious and unsure about whether I could be successful. I would spend the first grading period proving to myself that I could master the material. Once I did, I fell back into my unnoticed pattern of underachievement. During those first few years, my grandmother was called on numerous occasions about my behavior on the playground, yet no teacher ever confronted me or contacted my grandmother about the decline in my grades. It was evident that they thought I was doing "fine" and as long as I was not a "behavioral problem," there was no need to do anything differently.

In fourth grade I was placed in Ms. Peoples' class. She was a middle-aged, no-nonsense, proud African American woman. From day one she insisted on excellence from all of her students, and very specifically and unequivocally informed me that she knew who I was and she was not going allow me to be lazy and under-achieving. I was going to leave her class at the end of the year having been challenged and having developed confidence in my ability to succeed. She pushed me everyday to do better. If I slacked off, I stayed after school until I completed whatever it was I needed to finish. She called my grandmother a lot. Ms. Peoples was the first and only teacher at my elementary school to ever call my grandmother about my academic performance. As far as she was concerned, what I had been doing prior to entering her class was quite simply unacceptable and she was going utilize whatever resources she had, including involving my grandmother, to make it different. Ms. Peoples was also the first person in my life to explain to me what college was and to suggest that college could be a part of my future.

Another lesson Ms. Peoples made certain I learned was that as a Black child, people were going to think I was stupid, were going to expect bad things from me, and would put obstacles in the way of my success. My job, she said, was to work hard, believe in myself, and to never give up, even when it seemed like things were impossible. Failure was not an option. I recall returning to my elementary school many times during my junior high and high school years to speak to Ms. Peoples, specifically to be reminded that I was smart and that I had potential.

Whiteness as Property

This tenet of CRT, as discussed by Cheryl Harris, Law Professor and author of *Whiteness as Property*, suggests that *the origins of property rights in the United States are rooted in racial domination. The construction of white identity and the ideology of racial hierarchy were intimately tied to the evolution and expansion of the system of chattel slavery. The law has played a considerable role in transforming the abstract concept of race into something people believe is real and tangible, and has led to racialized privilege – where white racial identity provides the basis for allocating societal benefits. As a result of the history of race and racism in the United States and the role of the law, whiteness can be considered a property interest.* (DeCuir and Dixson, 2004)

I was a kid who loved math. Prior to entering fifth grade, Ms. Peoples convinced me that I could grow up to be a Math teacher. In eight grade, I was placed in a gifted Algebra class. I was the only brown-skinned student in the class. From the moment I walked into the class I knew the teacher didn't like me and that she didn't think I belonged in her class. She never smiled at me. She never called on me when I raised my hand. I would get sent to the office if I blurted out an answer and she rarely had time to answer my questions. Needless to say, I became a behavioral challenge in her class. As far as I was concerned, if she didn't care to include me in the educational process of her class, I was going to disrupt her class. I was removed from her class at the end of the semester with a close to failing grade. I was angry and discouraged. I did not take another math class until tenth grade, when I repeated Algebra.

In the following year when the school tried to put me in another gifted class, I refused. I was clear that I was not going to put myself in a position to be mistreated and made to feel inadequate ever again. I spent a lot of time trying to figure out what I did wrong and why she didn't like me. I finally concluded that she just believed that I didn't belong in her class. I didn't fit the profile of the student who should be taking gifted Algebra: I wasn't white.

We continue to see the same perspective manifested in our schools today. I worked with a school district to look at the disproportionality in their AP/GATE and Leadership courses district-wide. What we found, while not surprising, was incredibly disheartening. In a relatively diverse district, with 598 students taking AP courses, there was only one Black student in AP. There were significantly more Latino students enrolled in AP, however, they were all almost exclusively taking AP Spanish. When it was suggested that the school sites needed to take affirmative steps to ensure access to a higher quality, rigorous curriculum for all students, it was stated that the teachers believe that by opening up their classes, they will necessarily have to decrease the rigor of the course, which isn't fair to the students who belong there.

Translation: the brown skinned students don't belong in AP classes and if we let them in, the quality of the course will suffer, which isn't fair to the students who are "entitled" to be there. Sadly, not much has changed in 40+ years.

In law school all students have to take Property Law. As with most law classes, we have to examine the evolution of the concept of property over time. Inevitably we get to the era where the courts are grappling with the property law issue of restrictive covenants. One would think that when the class examines the court's reasoning in holding that the restrictive covenant, which prevented Blacks from purchasing property in certain areas, is valid, that the conversation would lead naturally to a discussion of the social issues of the time that led to the court validating inherently racist laws.

My Property Law professor liked his class orderly and predictable. He practiced the Socratic method and gave you the heads up when it was going to be your turn to perform. What he didn't like was being asked questions, particularly questions which required discussion of issues not specifically addressed in the court's reasoning, like race. The entire class knew that if you asked a question, you risked becoming the focus of his Socratic process, even if it was not your day to be on. Through this practice, he effectively silenced any discussions that would have identified and addressed the discrimination and oppression of people of color perpetuated by the law. However, I was unwilling to be silenced. I came to class over-prepared and ready to do battle and I challenged him everyday. As I began to grasp how completely entrenched racism is in our society and how the law has legitimized and validated racist practices for centuries, I became enraged and refused to allow yet another white teacher tell me that racism does not exist or that I am over-reacting or over-sensitive.

During my second year of law school, I had the honor and pleasure of spending an entire day with Professor Patricia J. Williams, author of *The Alchemy of Race and Rights: A Diary of a Law Professor*, and her then infant son, escorting them around the island of Oahu. During that roughly six hours, I shared with her my experience of being the only Black student in the entire law school. I shared how it felt to sit in a class like my property law class and have what continue to be my experiences with racism invalidated and to not have an ally willing to stand with me and challenge the professors limited interpretation of the law. Professor Williams was sympathetic and encouraging.   After almost 20 years I still remember her description of how she teaches her Property Law Class. Professor Williams begins the first session of her property law class by introducing a copy of the bill of sale for her grandmother.

What a powerful social statement! Can you imagine how different my property law experience would have been with a professor who was willing to not only identify the issue of institutionalized racism, but who also encouraged and engaged her students in an open and honest discourse on the subject?

Educators need to ensure that the message given to students of color is that they are not only welcomed in school, including the school's rigorous courses, but that their presence is desired and necessary to the well-being of our society as a whole. Rigor is not the property of white students. Furthermore, teachers must consciously consider how their teaching styles may stifle critical thinking, engagement and learning for all students, and particularly for students of color.

The Permanence of Racism

This CRT tenet, as explained by Derrick Bell and Charles Lawrence, both Law Professors and credited among the originators of CRT, suggests that *racism is a permanent component of American life and that racist hierarchical structures govern all political, economic, and social domains, including schools.* (DeCuir and Dixson, 2004) As much as we would like to believe that we live in a post-racial society, the reality is that race continues to influence all aspects of American life. To ignore this reality will only perpetuate the adverse impact racism has on our society.

At the age of 12, a parent of a friend took me to my first college women's basketball game. It happened to be a UCLA game. I had taken up playing basketball about a year earlier and apparently demonstrated some talent in the sport.

The parent thought it would be a good experience for me to see a college game to get an idea of the level of play and shared with me that the players on the team received scholarships to play basketball to pay for their college educations.

Ms. Peoples had already planted the seed about college during fourth grade and now I had identified a means to pay for my college education doing something I loved. I was so excited that I returned to my elementary school shortly after watching the UCLA game to share my news with Ms. Peoples and one other teacher I had become quite fond of while in elementary school. I will call this other teacher Ms. Stewart, who was probably a late thirty-something white woman. Ms. Stewart had also been a teacher who would not accept my lackadaisical performance and encouraged me to be a better student.

On the day I returned to my elementary school, I ran into Ms. Stewart first and I shared with her my great news with all of the enthusiasm of a 12 year old that had made a significant discovery; I was going to UCLA on a basketball scholarship and I was going to be a math professor. She looked at me very sympathetically, put her hand on my shoulder and told me that maybe UCLA was not a realistic goal for me and that I should not set myself up for disappointment. She went on to tell me that maybe community college was a more realistic goal for me. Hearing those few words, I was completely demoralized. I ran away from her crying and angry. I didn't bother to seek out Mrs. Peoples on that visit; I just wanted to go home. I returned a couple of days later to see Mrs. Peoples and told her my now "not so great" news and I also told her what Ms. Stewart had said to me.

Mrs. Peoples was furious! She sat me down and told me that not only was my goal reasonable, it was attainable. She reassured me that I was bright enough to go to college and that if I worked hard enough on my basketball skills I could be good enough to get a college scholarship. She reminded me about what she had told me in fourth grade; that there would be white teachers who would believe that I was less capable just because of the color of my skin. Lastly, she reminded me that she was "here" for me and, whenever I began to question my ability to succeed, to just come see her. As I have said, I visited Mrs. Peoples a number of times during my secondary educational experience. I can also proudly say that I again returned to my elementary school, this time five years later, in April of 1984 to show Mrs. Peoples my signed National Letter of Intent to attend UCLA on a full scholarship for women's basketball.

When I entered UCLA as a freshman, there were three other first-year women basketball players entering at the same time - two were white and one was Japanese. We all had to take an English and a Math assessment to determine our courses for the Fall. My assessment results solidly placed me in English 1, the English course necessary to graduate, and Calculus. When it came time to determine my schedule, my coaches and the academic advisor for athletes decided that I should take English 1A, a precursor to English 1, and Pre-Calculus, even though both my English and Math assessment scores placed me in the higher-level courses. Their rationale was that college courses were more rigorous than high school and given my basketball commitments, they did not want me to get overwhelmed. However, all three of my freshmen teammates were put in the higher-level courses, even though I scored higher than two of them in Math and our English scores were comparable. The coaches and advisor apparently didn't have the same concerns regarding course rigor and the potential for getting overwhelmed for the white and Asian basketball players.

Another requirement for all incoming freshman athletes was two hours per week of mandatory tutoring in both English and Math (whether you needed it or not) and mandatory daily study hall. Again, the coaches and the academic advisor decided that I needed six hours per week of English tutoring, three times as much as the other freshman athletes. They based this determination on what was admittedly a dismal SAT English score of 380. However, they completely ignored the results of the college English assessment I had just taken, which showed that my English skills were more advanced than what was represented by my SAT English score. They also refused to listen to my explanation for having obtained the low English score. (And, I did have an explanation. But that is a story for another time.) They again decided that they knew what was best for me and ignored any information I provided them to the contrary.

After several weeks of meeting with me six hours per week, my English tutor was clear that the amount of time was excessive and counterproductive. My English tutor was a Latina with an advanced degree in English, and when she scheduled a meeting with my coaches to explain that my English skills were advanced and did not require the current level of remediation, they were rude and dismissive towards her. They basically told her that her job was to tutor me, not to advise them, and that they would decide what was appropriate for me. When I refused to continue with the six hours of English tutoring, I was labeled "defiant." I took the remedial English and Math courses and I passed them both. No surprise!

By my second year at UCLA I had declared my

Math major and was entering the third level calculus course for Math and Engineering majors. At UCLA they have two tracks for Math, one for Math majors and Engineers and one for everyone else. I was the only Black female student in the class. My professor for this class was an older white man, with a long white beard, who stood on the stage and lectured for 1.5 hours. He did not allow questions during the lecture and if you had questions, you had to ask his teaching assistants, who were also white and male, during their limited office hours.

I don't know about anyone else, but listening to someone lecture nonstop for 1.5 hours about polar coordinates and other complicated mathematical concepts without the opportunity to put the material in context with questions, does not lead to comprehension. When I questioned the professor's teaching style and explained that it made it difficult for me to learn the concepts, the teaching assistant questioned my capacity to learn the material and told me that he didn't believe that I belonged in this class.

How many times do you think teachers have questioned the capacity or competency of their students because the students could not learn from their particular style of teaching?

It is essential that educators recognize the permanence and pervasiveness of racism. Because it is only with deliberate and conscious action to reject the status quo and to challenge low expectations for students of color that change in the form of improved achievement will be possible.

Interest Convergence/Material Determinism

This CRT tenet, as discussed by Derrick Bell, suggests that *communities of color will experience gains when they converge with the self-interest of whites.* The example I use to illustrate this tenet is actually not a personal story, but one of my favorite stories.

The movie *Glory Road* tells the story of Coach Don Haskins from Texas Western, now the University of Texas El Paso (UTEP), during the 1965-66 college basketball season. At this time in history, it was common for college basketball teams to have one or two Black athletes on the team. The rhetoric of the time was that you couldn't play more than one or two Blacks at a time because they didn't have the mental capacity to understand the strategy necessary to win basketball games. Because of their athleticism, they could contribute the "brawn," but it was the white players that had the brains necessary to win championships.

Coach Haskins was starting his first year as a college coach. He wanted to win, so he went out and recruited the best basketball players. It just so happens that the best basketball players were Black, and much to the dismay of the college and the boosters, he recruited seven of them. When his employer first learned about all the "negroes" he had recruited, Coach Haskins was told that his job was in jeopardy. The college community refused to support the team and often taunted and heckled the players during the games.

However, this was truly an extraordinary team, and not because they were Black, but because they were exceptionally talented. They went on to defeat most of the top-ranked teams in the country, all of whom still only had one or two Black athletes on their rosters. As the team chalked up win after win, and it became clear that they would be in contention for the national championship, the fans, the boosters, the college bureaucrats all came out en masse to support the team and to congratulate Coach Haskins for his brilliance. Recognizing that what had started out as a simple quest to win some basketball games, had become part of a larger civil rights and social justice movement, Coach Haskins made his second decision that would literally change the face of college sports forever: he started and played only the Black athletes during the nationally televised NCAA National Championship game. And they won.

Following this historic year, many colleges began to actively recruit Black athletes, not because it provided educational opportunities to a marginalized group in society, not because it was the right thing to do, but because with Black athletes they too might win a national championship.

Interest convergence suggests that meaningful initiatives to increase achievement of students of color will only occur when there is a benefit to white students. Educators are therefore encouraged to promote improved achievement for students of color even when there is no articulable benefit to white students.

Critique of Liberalism

This CRT tenant suggests that *liberalism as a framework for addressing America's racial problems, specifically, colorblindness, the neutrality of law, and incremental change, are insufficient to create meaningful change. Because racism is embedded in our thought processes and social structures, aggressive, color-conscious efforts are required to change the way things are.* (Delgado and Stefancic, 2012)

In my work with educators throughout California, I often hear comments like, "I don't see color," "we apply the rules equally to everyone," and "we need to roll this out over the next few years to allow the teachers to buy into the work." What the commenters fail to realize is that while these responses may seem ideal, all of these responses fail to consider the persistence of racism and the "oppressive nature of the normativity of Whiteness." (DeCuir and Dixson, 2004)

Take, for instance, the comment, "I don't see color," which is actually in direct conflict with current research results. In 2016, the Yale Child Study Center published *Implicit Bias in Preschool: A Research Study Brief*, which found that implicit biases take the form of subtle, sometimes subconscious stereotypes held by white teachers, which had been shown to result in lower expectations and rates of gifted program referrals for black students. The research team used an eye-tracking technology, which showed that preschool teachers "show a tendency to more closely observe black students, and especially boys, when challenging behaviors are expected." This research completely debunks the notion that teachers do not see color. Teachers may not be aware that they are subconsciously "seeing color," but they are in fact "seeing color" and acting on it, to the detriment of their students of color.

Similarly, applying rules "equally" is not necessarily "equitable." Equal application of rules ignores the reality of the impact of implicit bias on who is observed misbehaving. It dismisses the significance of racism, in its multitude of forms - micro-aggressions, conscious and unconscious racism, and implicit and explicit bias - and its impact on student behavior. When educators fail to examine student behavior on a case-by-case basis and fail to fairly exercise their discretion, which is what the law intends, they unwittingly perpetuate the racial disparities that exist.

Lastly, the idea that "incremental change" is necessary and appropriate to obtain "buy-in" by the majority is a wonderful concept when you and/or your child are not the ones who have to wait for the institutionalized structures to change in order to have your needs met. This token commitment to diversity often leads to the creation of "diversity" positions designed to address racism superficially. They are typically held by one of the only people of color in the institution, with very little support or resources, all of which is ultimately a recipe for failure. From a student's perspective, it often leads to the social isolation of those students of color deemed "exceptional enough" to have the honor of placement in a rigorous course, only to find they are the only one, or in a tiny minority, and apparently the expert for their race when topics regarding race and racism come up in class.

The liberal response to the #BlackLivesMatter Movement ("BLM") is a perfect example of why liberalism is an insufficient framework for addressing America's (and by extension, our schools') racial problems. The amount of people who where offended by BLM and insisted that #BlueLivesMatter and #AllLivesMatter illustrates why waiting for the majority to "buy-in" is not a practical solution. These folks missed the point: that BLM was in direct response to the social reality of Black men and women being murdered for being Black and the fact that these murders were "excused" because of the societal stereotypes that exclaim that Blacks are dangerous, must be feared, and, therefore, controlled by any means necessary.

People could not tolerate the focus on Black Lives. This focus on Black Lives somehow meant, to them, that other lives were not important, maybe even that their lives were not important. Thus they needed to push back and yell that #AllLivesMatter. Consequently, when a student presented an art project on BLM, the teacher and school administrator prohibited it from being displayed with the art projects of the other students, citing that it was divisive and recommending that a message of #AllLivesMatter would be acceptable. This response effectively shut down the student's constitutionally protected right to free speech and sent a message that the very real racial inequities that this student was trying to address through his art were not important.

We need schools that understand and appreciate that race is embedded in our thought processes and social structures and only with deliberate intention to change the status quo, which includes committing sufficient human and fiscal resources, will we be able to change the prevailing narrative about who our students of color are and what they are capable of.

Improving Student Achievement Through the Creation of Relationships

I have already introduced you to Ms. Kent and Ms. Peoples. I will now introduce you to a few more educators that were instrumental in helping me navigate the educational and personal challenges I faced. The thing they all have in common is that they all cared enough to look beyond the surface and get to know me. They recognized my potential and made it their business, indeed their job, to help me succeed.

Dennis Flynn, Lois Keithley and Pam Easter were all staff at my middle school in Los Angeles. Mr. Flynn, a white man, was my P.E. teacher and in many ways a surrogate parent. When I was in pain and needed a root canal in 8th grade and had no money and no insurance to pay for it, he lent me money without hesitation and based solely on my word that I would eventually pay him back.

When I began working from 5pm to 2am on

weeknights to help buy food and pay household bills, he gave me a cot to rest on at school, spoke with my teachers about my family challenges, and basically offered any assistance I needed to get my work completed and to manage my personal responsibilities.

When I was kicked off the girl's basketball team in 10th grade because the coach and I had personality conflicts, Mr. Flynn volunteered for the next two years as the assistant coach specifically to create a situation that would allow me to return to the team. He knew that the only way I was going to be able to afford college was on an athletic scholarship, and he wanted me to go to college.

Ms. Keithley, a white woman, was my grade-level academic counselor. When I came into her office and declared that I was going to UCLA and I needed to know what courses to take, she sat me down and developed a three-year schedule of classes with me that would prepare me for the high school courses I needed to take to get into UCLA. She never once questioned the appropriateness of my goal and was a constant source of encouragement when things in my personal life made my academic goals seem unattainable.

Ms. Easter, a Black woman, was a P.E. teacher at my middle school, but was never my teacher. Yet, she took an interest in me and became a mentor and an advisor to me - a role she continued to fill through my freshman year in college. In 9th grade I began developing an interest in softball. I always had to borrow equipment to play because I couldn't afford a glove or a bat. To encourage my continued participation, Ms. Easter bought me my first glove and bat as a graduation present.

Mr. Furlong, a white man, was my 11th grade Geometry teacher. He was also one of the football coaches and loved Black people. His comfort with his Black students was apparent in the way he spoke to us, interacted with us, and engaged us. It did not take him very long to recognize that I had an aptitude for math. Rather than let me continue my pattern of relative underachievement, he found ways to keep me motivated and engaged in his class. He eventually began having me periodically teach a class.

He would tell me what I needed to cover, give me the teacher's manual, and have me develop a lesson plan for the class. We would then review and edit the lesson plan as needed and I would teach the class. Mr. Furlong made math fun and his faith in my ability allowed me to rekindle the passion for math I had lost while taking gifted Algebra in 8th grade.

Eric Yamamoto, a Japanese man, was my professor in law school for several classes. He taught us the legal concepts we needed to learn by using materials that told the stories of the lives of the people the law impacted. He made the law relevant to our daily lives. Professor Yamamoto also created courses that directly addressed the racial justice and injustice in the law and provided a forum for dialogue regarding these issues.

One such class was *Race, Culture, and the Law*. The course began by defining Race and Racism then examined topics such as slavery and reconstruction, Jim Crow segregation and violence, the civil rights movement, indigenous peoples, immigration and citizenship, and racial reparations. Professor Yamamoto's courses provided a meaningful and culturally relevant alternative to the traditional legal education that often left me feeling invisible and further marginalized.

Mrs. Williams, a Black woman, was a clerk in the attendance office at my high school. Somehow she knew that my sister and I did not have parents at home and were essentially on our own. Every time I came into the attendance office, she always greeted me with a smile, she always asked how I was doing (not cringing when the answer was "not great") and she was always attentive to whatever my particular need was that brought me into the office. Through her kindness, she conveyed that she saw me and cared about my circumstances.

Violet Palmer, a Black woman, was the first female NBA official. While she did not work in schools, she was an adult in my life who understood the importance of creating spaces for women and girls, particularly women and girls of color, to come together, push each other, and be lifted up by each other. Back in the late 80s, before she was an NBA official, she was the director of Baldwin Hills Recreation Center in Los Angeles. While in that position, Ms. Palmer created opportunities for women and girls to play basketball at a high level of competition, before expensive AAU and Club teams, and at a time when there was not a lot of energy going into women's sports.

Ms. Palmer was a constant source of inspiration and encouragement. I remember when I first started going to the open gym, I was younger than many of the other players and still improving. As a result, I was a bit intimidated and unsure of whether I belonged there. Ms. Palmer made it clear to me that I was welcome and could be competitive with the other women. She encouraged me to keep my head up and to continue to work hard. It was clear that Ms. Palmer's philosophy was the sky was the limit and with hard work and perseverance, I could achieve my goals, even in a society that seemed to focus on my limitations imposed by racial stereotypes. Every adult who interacts with children needs to understand (and possibly be reminded) that they have the power to positively influence their lives just by showing care and kindness.

The reason these educators stand out is because they understood that teaching begins with the establishment of a relationship with the student. They knew me, and who I was outside of school was just as important to them as the student I was in the classroom.

A few years ago, I conducted Saturday training with elementary school teachers on race and how their personal histories and beliefs influenced their perceptions and expectations for student learning. During our follow-up session 3 weeks later, one of the teachers shared that during the first day of training she kept finding herself thinking about one particular Black boy in her class and wondering how her expectations may be contributing to his behavioral problems. She shared that she spent a significant amount of her time addressing his behavior. She had grown accustomed to his disruptions and she had begun ignoring him as a way to try to deter his behavior.

The Monday following the training, rather than ignore him, she greeted him at the door and asked him how his weekend was. After his initial shock from the fact that his teacher had actually addressed him for something other than a disciplinary reason, he broke into a huge smile and proceeded to tell her all about his weekend. Everyday since, this student has approached her and shared something with her about his time after school. The teacher happily reported that his behaviors in class have decreased significantly as a result of him beginning to feel connected to her.

Another reason my educators stand out is because they had high expectations for my learning and development, even when I didn't always have high expectations for myself. They did not settle for, nor did they allow me to be content with, under-achievement. They challenged me to be a better student and a better person.

In another district where we were looking at disproportionality in the GATE program, one of the administrators assigned his GATE teacher to teach the same course to non-GATE students. She is teaching the exact same content, with some differentiation of instruction, and guess what - the non-GATE students are learning the more rigorous material. Imagine what would happen if teachers didn't blame poor student achievement on their parents, or their poverty, or their culture, but expected that all students could achieve at high levels and then helped them believe in their own ability to achieve. We would have students that felt cherished and engaged and would be ultimately well-educated.

Another school I worked with had approximately 8% African American students and they did not have any African American teachers. The only African American on staff was a custodian. The administration was noticing the disproportionate rate of discipline of the Black students as well as the fact that they were less connected to the predominately white staff. In addition to supporting the staff in improving their connections with the Black students, the administration consulted with the custodian and asked if he would be willing to be a presence during recess and lunch and interact with the students, with a focus on the Black students. He engaged with the students by shooting hoops, checking in, and throwing balls, in an effort to help them feel more connected. Within the first month, the custodian knew the names of all the Black students and had begun developing relationships with them, helping them feel more connected to school. Referrals for misbehaviors on the playground decreased.

In 2015, I had the honor of being inducted into the Los Angeles City Section Hall of Fame. The overwhelming feeling I had was that life had gone full circle. I was no longer the stubborn, angry and introverted kid that started this journey 50 years before. As I gave my acceptance speech - reflecting on the obstacles I overcame and the things I'd achieved both athletically and professionally – I looked out to the guest sitting at my table: Mr. Flynn, Ms. Easter and Mr. Miyata still supporting and encouraging me after 37 year. Their continued presence in my life is truly the epitome of the importance and transformative impact of building relationships with your students.

In order to improve the academic achievement, and general well-being for students of color, educators must first acknowledge, then examine, the significance of politics, economics, and race on the educational experiences of and opportunities for students of color in schools. By thinking critically about these social conditions, the impact on the educational experiences of students of color, and how their care can transform the lives of their students, educators can begin to create opportunities for equity and higher levels of achievement for all students.

I will leave you with a quote from Lisa Delpit's book, *Other People's Children: Cultural Conflict in the Classroom*.

"The purpose of education is to learn to die satiated with life… What we need from our schools are experiences that are so full of the wonder of life, so full of connectedness, so embedded in the context of our communities, so brilliant in the insights that we develop and the analyses that we devise, that all of us, teachers and students alike, can learn to live lives that leave us truly satisfied."

CRT GRAPHIC ORGANIZER

A Critical Race Theory Counter-Story

The following graphic organizer is a tool to help you think about and structure what the tenets of CRT mean to you and how they apply to your personal and professional life. I hope you will take some time to engage in this exercise and reflect on what your narrative might look like.

CRT Theme	Theoretical What does the tenet mean in layperson's terms?
What, When, Why?	
Counter-Storytelling	
The Permanence of racism	
Whiteness as Property	
Interest Convergence	
Critique of Liberalism	

CRT Theme	Personal CRT in my life?
What, When, Why?	
Counter-Storytelling	
The Permanence of racism	
Whiteness as Property	
Interest Convergence	
Critique of Liberalism	

CRT Theme	Professional Application of the tenet in my work?
What, When, Why?	
Counter-Storytelling	
The Permanence of racism	
Whiteness as Property	
Interest Convergence	
Critique of Liberalism	

CRT Theme	Organizational Evidence of this tenet in my organization?
What, When, Why?	
Counter-Storytelling	
The Permanence of racism	
Whiteness as Property	
Interest Convergence	
Critique of Liberalism	

About the Author

Dora J. Dome, Esq.

Dora J. Dome, Esq. has practiced Education Law for over 23 years, primarily in the areas of student issues and special education. She graduated from University of Hawaii, Richardson School of Law (J.D.) and from University of California, Los Angeles (B.A.).

In 2016, she published her first book, *Student Discipline, Special Education Discipline, Anti-Bullying and Other Relevant Student Issues: A Guide For Practitioners*, which has been described as a "must-have" for anyone seeking to understand student discipline and bullying. In 2017, Ms. Dome published her second book, *Understanding Student Discipline in California Schools: A Parent's Guide to General and Special Education Discipline*, to assist parents in navigating the school discipline process. This book has also been translated into Spanish! In 2020, Ms. Dome published her fourth and fifth books, respectively, *Student Discipline Resource Binder: A Comprehensive Guide for K-12 Schools,* and

Improving Student Achievement Through The Creation of Relationships: A Critical Race Theory Counter-Story. Both books are part of her new series called **Tools For The Trade.**

Ms. Dome currently provides legal representation to school districts on student issues and develops and conducts professional development trainings for district staff that focus on Bullying and Legal Compliance, viewed through an Equity Lens, in a proactive effort to build staff capacity to address the changing needs of their students.

Admitted to the Hawaii State Bar in 1996, Ms. Dome served as a special education consultant and trainer for the Hawaii State Department of Education and Hawaii State Department of Health for five years. Ms. Dome was admitted to the California Bar in 2003. She worked with the education law firm of Dannis Woliver Kelley, (fka Miller Brown and Dannis) for eight years.

Ms. Dome has studied in the areas of Race and Ethnicity, Critical Legal Studies and Critical Race Theory and has been certified as a Cultural Diversity Trainer by the National Coalition Building

Institute (aka NCBI). She has developed and conducted trainings for numerous school districts and school boards in the areas of student diversity and equity, student and special education discipline, harassment/discrimination, bullying, special education, trauma sensitive schools, alternative assessments for African American students, Section 504, and student records.

Ms. Dome also regularly presents at association conferences such as ACSA, CSBA and CASCWA. She participated on the Gay & Lesbian Athletics Foundations (aka GLAF) Keynote Panel on "Race and Racism in LGBT Athletics" and presented at the NCAA Black Coaches Association Annual Conference on "Homophobia in Sports."

Ms. Dome is a Lecturer at the University of California at Berkeley, teaching Education Law and Policy in Principal Leadership Institute (PLI) Program. She was also an Adjunct Professor at Mills College teaching in the administrative credential program for soon to be administrators.

Made in the USA
Columbia, SC
23 July 2020